Your Body Y

Edited by Scilla Dyke MBE

Contents

Published by Dance UK
Battersea Arts Centre
Lavender Hill
London SW11 5TN

www.danceuk.org

Dancers are artists and athletes. Their talent brings inspiration, creativity and pleasure to audiences everywhere. These achievements are hard-won, the result of years of intensive training, determination and continual physical challenge. Achieving and maintaining peak performance also requires knowledge if dancers are to balance a demanding work schedule with a healthy lifestyle.

I welcome *Your Body Your Risk* as an important source of advice and help for dancers. Knowledge is power, and this booklet has the power to keep you dancing. I wish you all a long and healthy dancing career.

The Rt Hon Tessa Jowell MP
Secretary of State for Culture, Media and Sport

Dance is about communicating, and being a dancer is about finding and learning ways to express your unique identity. To dance you need to be your own person. You need to make your own choices and do what feels right for you and your body.

To be a dancer you need commitment and dedication, discipline and focus. But you also need to be true to yourself and believe in yourself. Physically you need to be fit and healthy, not constantly struggling with your weight or spending all your time worrying about what you eat.

You need a healthy attitude to your own well-being.

As you go through your dance training and your subsequent career, a lot of demands will be made on you physically, mentally and emotionally.

There will be pressure to succeed from all sides; from friends, teachers and choreographers, maybe even from your parents, family or friends. You may feel that their love, encouragement, support and respect depends upon your success. You need to remember that it's impossible to please everyone. You can't always live up to other people's expectations. If you try to, you will wear yourself out and you could damage your health in the attempt.

"Prioritising your attention and commitment to maintaining a healthy body and mind is critical to exceptional performance - on stage, in rehearsal, whilst teaching, even in discussion. Giving value to your body means giving the time to understand it and demands intelligent, informed and regular care."
Wayne McGregor

Dance training is intensely physical. Your body needs to be strong, powerful and well nourished to perform. If you continually push yourself beyond your limits, your body will be exhausted, and you are more likely to get ill or injured.

If you continually worry about your weight, always compare yourself to others, and believe the thinner you are the better you dance, then food will start to control your life. Constantly thinking about what you eat will stop you concentrating on what you love - dancing.

Men and women are both at risk from developing an eating disorder. It's a scary thought, but having an eating disorder may ultimately damage your career or even end your life.

Your Body Your Risk looks at ways you can deal with the pressures and problems you face as a dancer, and the dangers eating disorders can pose to your health and your career. It provides information and advice to help you take responsibility for your own well-being.

Take care of yourself. You're worth it.

Your body, your responsibility

Body talk

Body image

Put simply, your body image is how you see yourself and your body and your feelings towards it. It is an internal picture created through experiences and information you have collected since early childhood. How you view your body can affect how you interact with the world and make your way through life.

Your body image is very complex. It is constantly influenced by a number of factors:

- comments from teachers, choreographers, partners, family and friends
- how you interpret feedback given on your dancing
- your home life and family values
- the school you train in, the classes you take, the artists and companies you work with
- the opinions of your friends and peers
- your cultural background

All of these help you form your own unique body image.

"Traditionally lithe, waif and skinny aren't a part of Asian beauty. There's no pressure to be thin. Asian dancers don't see any need to starve themselves. They also don't see their careers ending. But second generation dancers are becoming aware of body image."
Sujata Banerjee

Your body image isn't fixed. It changes with your age, experiences and general well-being. You may look in the mirror one day and feel great. On another occasion, you might not feel so good, and overestimate/underestimate your size or think that there is something wrong with a part of your body.

Growing and changing

During teenage years your body constantly changes. You grow rapidly; this is called the 'Growth Spurt'. You may get taller before your muscles can catch up, leaving you weaker than before. Or you may find that you are temporarily lopsided.

You may feel awkward or uncoordinated. Dramatic changes in your body's shape and size can make you feel helpless and out of control. Don't worry, this is normal. Eventually your body will regain *and increase* its strength and co-ordination. Many people go through a stage of feeling uncomfortable with their bodies in their teens and most grow out of this feeling naturally.

Remember that everyone grows at different rates and friends of the same age may look very different.

What do you want from your body?

Do you think you should be lithe, agile, and glowing with health and vitality?

Do you think dancers need powerful, strong bodies? Should men's bodies be lean, sinewy and defined? Should women's bodies be flat-chested with hips and collar bones showing?

Do you think dancers need to be thinner than other people? Is a thin body necessary for success?

Often dancers think thin is good, thinner is better, and thinnest is best. Even the fittest and most balanced dancers can be tempted to give in to pressures to lose just that little bit more weight. In some dance forms, for example ballet, the pressure to be thin may be imposed on you by the expectations of teachers, artistic directors, choreographers and audiences. In such situations, you need to work harder to keep a healthy perspective.

As a dancer, your body image can become entwined with how you value yourself. In your attempt to carve out a dancing career, you may overestimate the size of your body, believing you're larger than you actually are. If you are obsessed with getting thinner and set unachievable goals for yourself, you will be increasingly insecure about your body, and your dancing.

Remember - your success as a dance artist depends upon your personality and your artistry, your technical ability and your performance power - not on how thin you are.

"I became drawn to work in which I have a voice in the process, devising and collaborating. I am respected for what I as a whole person bring to the work and not judged on how my body looks."
Christine Devaney

How do you see yourself?
Find out what your body is really like.

Lie on the floor. Sense your body on the ground. Which parts are heavy? Which are light? Where are you broad or narrow? Which parts of your body do you like and/or dislike?

Relax and take time to think about this.

Slowly get up. Draw the outline of your image of your body on the ground using coloured chalk *guessing* your height, width, curves and musculature. Once you have finished, look at what you have drawn.

Next, lie down on the image you have created. Then get someone else to draw round your body using another colour. Carefully get up and look at the difference between the two outlines.

What do you notice?

The chances are you'll be surprised. You're probably thinner than you think. Why not talk to a friend about what you've discovered about yourself and your body by doing this exercise?

If you're worried

Do you dislike the way you look? Do you use the mirrors in the dance studio to check your alignment, or do you use the mirror to add to your sense of dissatisfaction with the shape of your body?

Perhaps you could try to focus on enjoying the physical sensation of dancing, on how your body feels rather than how you think it looks. You could ask your teachers to take some parts of the class facing away from the mirrors, and try focusing *through* the mirror rather than *on* it. This will help you to develop your ability to communicate through your dancing too.

If you are really worried about your body shape you may be unsure about what to do. You may hate the way you look. You may spend too much time thinking about your body. Perhaps you recognise some of these signs in a classmate or company member.

If you are concerned, you should talk to someone that you feel comfortable with who can give you advice. *(See 'What can I do now?')*

Body balance

Every dancer has their own optimum weight for health and performance. But how do you know if you are the right weight?

A quick way to check if you are a healthy weight is to work out your 'body mass index' (BMI).

Take your weight in kilos e.g. 60k

Divide it by your height (in metres) squared e.g. 1.66 m x 1.66m = 2.75

60 / 2.75 = 21.8 BMI

And the result?

FEMALE DANCERS

BMI

19 – 25
This is the level recommended for good health. Over 25 BMI is overweight, over 30 moves into obesity and can present a health risk.

17.5 – 19
This is below the recommended level. Many dancers' BMIs fall in this range. If you have a BMI of under 19 but still have periods, it's OK. If your periods have stopped your bones may be at risk. *(See 'Bone wise')*

17.5 and under
This is very underweight

MALE DANCERS

BMI

20 – 25
This is the level recommended for good health. You can still be healthy with a BMI higher than this.

Under 20
Your BMI may be below 20 until you stop growing, but if it stays there as a result of under-eating you are at risk of low testosterone levels and weak bones. *(See 'Bone wise')*

Your BMI is only a guide. It takes into account a total of all the components of your body: bone, muscle mass and body fat. It is most useful as an indication of being under-weight.

Eating for health and performance

How would you describe healthy eating?

Eating when you're hungry, stopping when you're full? Three regular, balanced meals a day? And what about indulging or overeating on special occasions such as birthdays or festivals? Dancers don't always get the chance to eat meals at regular times, but this doesn't mean that your eating isn't healthy or that you're automatically suffering from disordered eating.

The truth about what to eat

As a dancer you need a healthy diet to maximise your energy stores, boost your immune system and enable you to train more effectively. By eating healthily, you will feel less tired and reduce the risk of becoming ill or being injured.

One way to ensure that you are eating healthily is to create a 'performance eating plan' designed - by you - to give you the necessary energy and nutrients to meet the rigours of your training and performing schedule. This doesn't mean spending hours deciding what to 'allow' or 'not allow' yourself to eat.

If you don't eat enough, you'll feel hungry and you'll spend more time thinking about food than anything else in your life. If you eat the right things and follow your performance eating plan, thoughts about food won't dominate your life. You can then get on with dancing and living.

Your Performance Eating Plan

A pattern of regular meals and snacks is best. But we're not talking about crisps, sweets, chocolates and fizzy drinks. Many snack foods are low in essential nutrients. This doesn't mean you can never eat crisps or sweets, just that they should be a very small part of your eating plan. Dancers need a high quality diet.

Energy boosting meals
Power packed meals should include:

Protein   meat, poultry, fish, eggs, cheese, pulses or tofu.

PLUS

starchy carbohydrates   cereal, bread, pasta, rice or potatoes.

You should also eat at least five portions of fruit, salad or vegetables every day.

Supercharged snacks

- fruit (fresh or dried)
- for a more substantial snack - cereal bars, fruit buns, malt loaf, scones or a small sandwich
- low fat milks and yoghurts are great sources of calcium (which is good for your bones)

Your diet should be low fat but not 'no fat'. As fats contain essential fatty acids (which play a role in the immune system and blood clotting amongst other things) and also allow you to absorb vitamins A,D,E and K. A low fat diet allows you to fit in more energy giving carbohydrates.

Fluid intake
Dehydration won't improve your performance. In fact quite the opposite; it can lead to muscle cramps and injury and severely affect your ability to dance. Drinking less around a performance may enhance feelings of lightness, but it will reduce your ability to perform well. You should drink at least 1 1/2 litres of water a day; before, during and after rehearsals, classes and performances.

Menu planning for your Performance Eating Plan

The following are just some suggestions of nutrient-packed meals. Portion sizes are for guidance only – if you are making healthy choices you can generally rely on your appetite to guide you on quantities. Judging the right amount is also easier if you don't eat too quickly – people who eat quickly don't get the 'full' signals in time to stop before they are over-full!

BREAKFAST

Choose one or more from:

1-2 Weetabix with semi-skimmed milk and a sliced banana.

A bowl of Shreddies/Flakes with semi-skimmed milk and chopped oranges – fresh or canned.

4-6 tablespoons muesli with yoghurt and chopped apple.

1-2 slices wholemeal bread spread with a little butter/margarine and some honey/jam/marmalade.

A toasted bagel with low fat soft cheese & chives.

A small tin of baked beans on 1-2 slices toast.

A toasted teacake (try wholemeal ones) with a little spread and jam/honey.

Feel free to swap suggested fruits around – there are no 'miracle' combinations and any choice is giving you vital nutrients. If you're not having fruit, try a glass of juice instead.

It's fine to drink some tea or coffee with this – white coffee is more 'bone-friendly' than black coffee – but keep it to a cup/mug unless it's caffeine free. Or try fruit/herb teas or fruit/vegetable juices instead.

LUNCHES

Sandwiches are a great choice for an easy lunch – wholemeal bread is best for vitamins, minerals and fibre, but try rye bread or other breads for variety. Include a source of protein and some vegetables/salad or fruit, for example:

Ham & tomato.

Tuna and cucumber (in spring water, oil or brine, and use a little salad cream or low fat dressing rather than mayonnaise).

Sliced hard boiled egg with tomato.

Grilled back bacon with lettuce & tomato.

Cottage cheese with pineapple.

Edam/Gouda cheese & salad.

Sliced brie/camembert & grapes.

Mozarella & sliced tomato.

Or make your own salad – a mixed salad with feta cheese and a bread roll, or pasta salad with tuna & sweetcorn or rice salad with tomato, peppers and diced ham, chicken or tuna.

If you can't keep salads or sandwiches in a fridge try a cool bag – warm sandwiches and salads are too risky for health.

Jacket potatoes with fillings are another good choice – add in some protein and some vegetables or a side salad for the best balance – e.g. tuna & sweetcorn, chicken curry, melted cheese, baked beans, cottage cheese (plain or with additions), chilli con carne (or vegetarian chilli).

Add a piece of fruit and the basics are there – if you need more, add in yoghurt or scone or teacake.

EVENING MEALS

These are essential to replenish energy levels after the day's demands. Plan to include a portion of potatoes (a medium jacket potato or its equivalent if having boiled/mashed), pasta or rice (50-75g uncooked is a good starting point for portion sizing). Potatoes are a source of Vitamin C – an anti-oxidant that is essential for healing, whilst brown rice and pasta supply B vitamins for healthy nerves and energy release. Add in some protein and vegetables/salad and the meal is balanced.

It can be as simple or elaborate as time and enthusiasm allow. Grilled (or try poached) chicken or fish with potatoes and vegetables (fresh or frozen are both great) or salad, makes a quick, easy and nourishing meal. Stir frying pork fillet, chicken or tofu with vegetables and noodles or rice is another good standby as is pizza (add vegetable toppings or serve with salad). At weekends, when you have more time, casseroles with meat or beans and vegetables served with potatoes are a good choice.

If you're eating out after a performance, your choices may be limited. Burgers and fish and chip shops are OK occasionally or in emergencies, but your body will benefit more from a meal that also includes vitamin and mineral rich vegetables or salads – whether it's cooked Chinese, Thai, Italian, French or Indian style. Choose dishes that you know won't be too oily.

Fruit and yoghurt are ideal desserts. Baked apples/pears/bananas or stewed fruit (fresh or dried) are alternatives to fresh fruit.

What's your diet like?

1 **How many portions of milk, cheese and yoghurt do you include each week?**
   (a) 1-6   (b) 7-13   (c) 14-21

2 **How many portions of meat, fish, eggs, soya products and beans do you include daily?**
   (a) 0-1   (b) 1-2   (c) 2-3

3 **How many portions of fruit, salad and vegetables do you eat each day?**
   (a)1-2   (b) 3-4   (c) 5-7

4 **Do you drink black tea/black coffee/cola?**
   (a) more than once daily   (b) occasionally   (c) never

5 **When the sun is shining are you**
   (a) going lobster coloured?
   (b) inside rehearsing/taking class?
   (c) making sure you get outside for brief periods but ensuring you don't burn?

6 **Does your weight**
   (a) change by more than 3 kg on a regular basis?
   (b) change by more than 3 kg each year?
   (c) stay fairly steady from month to month?

7 **Is your alcohol intake**
   (a) more than 30 units weekly?
   (b) 15-30 units weekly?
   (c) up to 14 units weekly?

SCORING
   a) 1 point   b) 3 points   c) 5 points

TOTAL SCORE

7-10	Time to review what you eat and make some changes for optimum health
11-20	Check out the questions where you scored less well and think about making some changes
21-33	This is a good score - but can you improve it?
34+	Excellent

For more information on nutrition for dance see Dance UK's Information Sheets 12 & 15.

Bone wise

Healthy bones are crucial to you as a dancer and to your long-term career. Your bones are a living tissue that you need to take care of for life. As strong as steel, and light enough to dance with, bone is brilliantly engineered scaffolding which supports the body against the forces of gravity and resists the pull of muscles to allow movement. Bones consist of connective tissue (collagen), calcium salts and other minerals which form a honeycomb structure.

Healthy bone

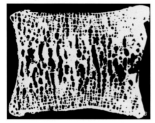

Osteoporotic bone

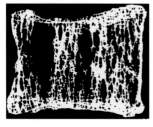

Your skeleton replaces itself every seven to ten years. By your mid-twenties it reaches its maximum strength and density. You need to look after your bones now if you want strong, healthy bones in later life.

Osteoporosis

If the holes in the honeycomb structure of your bones become bigger, the internal architecture changes, becoming fragile and liable to break easily. Your bones become thin and brittle and this is known as osteoporosis, or porous bones.

As a dancer you're at risk. Dance training with regular weight bearing exercise (exercise that exerts a loading impact and stretches and contracts the muscles) stimulates bone to strengthen. But you may be taking your bone health for granted. The combination of too much exercise (weight bearing or not) and too little food, causes oestrogen or testosterone levels to drop. Oestrogen (for women) and testosterone (for men) are crucial to the health of your skeleton.

Low oestrogen levels, and possibly testosterone levels, can seriously weaken your skeleton resulting in dangerously thin and brittle bones, even when you're young. Thin, brittle bones are prone to 'fragility fractures', where a minor bump or fall can cause a broken bone. Your bones can be weakened for life.

Women with low oestrogen are most at risk. Your best guide to low oestrogen levels in your body is when your periods stop. Your periods can stop as a consequence of intense training coupled with a diet low in energy. No periods for six months could result in low bone density and increased risk of fracture. Without periods the bones will lose density and the bones of a dancer in her twenties can become as weak as those of a 70 year-old.

If you're Afro-Caribbean the risk is genetically slightly less, because you have bigger, denser bones than Caucasians.

If you don't have periods for six months or more, seek medical advice from a GP or a family planning clinic. You may have a medical problem other than just your weight.

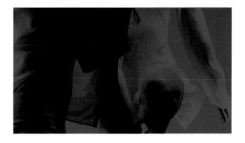

How do I know if I've got osteoporosis?

Osteoporosis is hidden until your first fracture. These fragility fractures can occur with very little force, perhaps as you land from a jump or even as you bend down to pick something up. These fractures can result in debilitating and potentially deforming injuries.

How to prevent weak bones

You need to take care of yourself now. Bones need food, exercise and healthy hormone levels. You need to balance your training, diet and body weight for maximum bone health.

Calcium is the most important mineral in your skeleton. You need to achieve a balance between your calcium intake and the amount of calcium lost from your body. To do this you need to make sure that you get enough calcium in your diet. Consuming dairy products is the easiest way to increase your calcium intake, but non-dairy foods also contain calcium.

Some factors increase your level of calcium absorption, such as high impact exercise, like dancing, running and skipping.

Some factors upset the balance of calcium absorption/loss, including high intakes of caffeine and salt.

You should aim to have a healthy lifestyle. Evidence shows that smoking and heavy drinking both damage your bone health.

Are you getting enough calcium?

If you are over sixteen, whether you are male or female,
your daily intake of calcium needs to be 1000 mg.

The following foods are good sources of calcium	Amount	Calcium mg
Dairy products		
Semi-skimmed milk	570 ml	702
Skimmed milk	570 ml	705
Reduced fat cheddar cheese	average in sandwich	410
Cottage cheese	100	73
Ice-cream (dairy)	average portion	134
Low-fat yoghurt	150g pot	225
Fromage frais (fruit)	100g	86
Parmesan cheese sauce	190 ml milk & 25g parmesan	541
Cheese & tomato pizza	average portion	235
Cheese omelette	100g	280
Fruit		
Apricots (dried)	4	73
Figs (dried)	100g	250
Orange	1 large	99
Vegetables		
Baked beans	450g tin	239
Baked potato	large	24
Broccoli, boiled	3 florets	54
Red kidney beans	small 220g tin	156
Spinach (boiled)	100g	160
Pulses, nuts & seeds		
Tofu steamed	100g	510
Almonds	100g	240
Brazil	100g	170
Peanuts (plain)	100g bag	60
Sesame seeds	2 tablespoons	134
Fish		
Pilchards in tomato sauce	100g	300
Sardines in tomato sauce	100g	460
Whitebait (fried)	100g	860
Cereals		
Wholemeal bread	1 slice	16
White bread	1 slice	33
Muesli	100g	110

Easy ways to boost your calcium intake:

- For breakfast have cereal & milk.
- As a snack have a yoghurt, some nuts or dried fruit.
- Use yoghurt-based salad dressing.
- Eat green vegetables such as broccoli, spinach, watercress and spring greens.

As a dancer your body is always on show. There can be a lot of pressure to be slim and to conform to an idealised, even an unrealistic, body image. You may feel that there are aspects of your life that are beyond your control, and that limiting what you eat gives you some sense of control over your life.

You may get a high from eating less. Or if you feel unhappy, you may eat too much and then make yourself sick, starve, over-exercise or use laxatives or diuretics in an effort to get rid of the excess calories.

Dancers have a high risk of developing disordered eating patterns. Disordered eating can creep up on you gradually and may lead to developing a serious eating disorder.

Do you spend too much time thinking about food? Do you think of it as something essential to your health and well-being? Do you think of food as a dangerous substance? Is it a taboo subject that you'd rather not think about?

Disordered eating or eating disorder?

Disordered eating encompasses a range of eating patterns and attitudes to food that ultimately result in you not getting a fully balanced diet. Disordered eating isn't an eating disorder and isn't necessarily dangerous to health, but if you display disordered eating patterns it puts you at a higher risk of developing a clinical eating disorder.

The ideal for us all is to eat well-balanced, nutritional food at regular intervals throughout the day. This is particularly difficult for dancers because of the practical demands of life as a dancer. It is easy to find yourself not eating properly.

Losing control

You may eat junk food because it's 'easier'. You may skip meals or eat at unusual times. It's easy to overlook the importance of having enough of the right food. You're training rigorously and there just isn't time to eat. You're too tired to go food shopping, or you're too busy rehearsing. You grab a coffee, a chocolate bar or some crisps, intending to eat properly later. You know this isn't a good pattern but it is not yet an eating disorder.

You might start to worry about the nutritional content of the food you are eating. You may try to make up for shortfalls by taking supplements. You may start to become obsessive about food, checking the content of everything you buy or attempting to cut out certain foods altogether.

It isn't healthy to spend the majority of each day worrying about what food you'll allow yourself to eat. For example, you may separate foods into 'good' or 'bad'. If eating a 'bad' food makes you feel guilty, it suggests that your eating is disordered. Most people don't fill their days this way. It's also unhealthy to avoid going out for a meal because you're worried about what might or might not be on the menu or the ingredients contained within the dishes. Constantly weighing your food (except when you're following a recipe) or worrying about the fat content of what you eat, can also be signs of disordered eating.

Missing meals when you don't need to, or only eating once a day, is neither normal nor healthy.

Research has shown clearly that disordered eating and dieting put you at risk of developing an eating disorder. Dancers show higher rates of eating disorders than the general population, but you need to give your body enough fuel to sustain high levels of physical exertion. You need a 'performance eating plan' to give you the energy you need. *(See 'Eating for health and performance')*

"Like many dancers, I went through ten years of problems with my weight - I was either thin and exhausted or... overweight. I was lucky – I met someone who explained to me how the body works, how food is used to provide energy and how some foods are more useful in that respect than others. I found a balance through an understanding of the facts. I eat lots and lots of the right things and keep the wrong, or less useful, things to a minimum."
Deborah Bull

Effects of disordered eating

FOR WOMEN

Period problems

If you're a dancer you'll be taking classes every day, plus rehearsing and performing. You'll probably be working out in the gym, swimming or doing Pilates or yoga. If you place these kinds of extreme physical demands on your body your periods may stop. This is even more likely to happen if your weight has dropped to below normal levels through dieting or disordered eating.

Many female dancers start their periods late. Once started, periods often stop. But you might think, 'So what? Periods can be rather inconvenient for a dancer'.

Hormones for health

Usually healthy women have regular periods, and regular periods are a sign of good health. If your periods stop for more than three months this is a medical condition called *amenorrhoea*.

If your periods stop then it may mean that you are not producing enough of the female hormone, oestrogen. Low oestrogen levels can lead to:

- low absorption of calcium into your bones which will lead to osteoporosis, this can cause broken bones and deformity *(see 'Bone wise')*
- painful sexual intercourse
- a low sex drive
- infertility

Not having periods doesn't just harm your body. It plays with your emotions too, and you need the strength of your body and your full personality as a woman to become the best dancer you can be.

Your periods can stop for a number of reasons. You could be suffering from stress, be experiencing one of a number of medical conditions or you may be pregnant. Whatever the cause, this is an important sign that you should not ignore. Seek advice from your GP.

FOR MEN

Male dancers are at risk too. If your shape and body weight fluctuate, your hormone levels drop. Low levels of the male hormone, testosterone, can cause:

- weakened bones *(see 'Bone wise')*
- a low sex drive
- infertility

Flirting with food

If you're in pursuit of the perfect body, you may start flirting with food. You may be tempted to diet sporadically or eat just enough to survive the rigours of training. You may feel you can't cope with the curves, bumps and emotions bombarding you as your body develops. Controlling your food intake may help you feel you are exercising control of your body.

As you work out elaborate ways of eating less you start to think about food all the time. You feel excited as your weight gets lower and lower. As you cut down on food, emergency brain chemicals kick in. You feel alive, have unexpected energy, your senses seem heightened. You feel great.

But what you are feeling is known as the 'starvation high', it doesn't last. It is your brain's way of helping you cope with the emergency situation of food deprivation. It isn't a true reflection of your body's energy stores. What this really means is that you are literally starving your body of what it needs. You are quite simply putting your future health and career at risk.

Flirting with disaster

If you don't eat enough to provide the energy that you need, you are forced to burn muscle and essential fat from your own body. This is self-destructive it can have long term consequences and may cause permanent damage.

The result? You lose stamina and get tired more quickly. Your concentration becomes poor and your bones thin. Injuries become more frequent and take longer to heal. If you are female your periods may stop. If you persist, you will be forced to stop dancing because you won't have the muscle power to lift your legs. You could even rupture your tendons, fracture your bones or tear your ligaments.

As you lose weight the chemical changes in your body and brain distort your thinking. It can seem as if the only thing you're good at is planning and controlling what you eat. Eventually, nothing matters except maintaining weight loss.

You have made food your enemy and you constantly worry that you will lose control and be unable to stop eating.

You may feel isolated, lonely and unable to cope. Perhaps it's your way of avoiding painful feelings or of keeping them under control. But what seemed like a solution has become itself a new and ever-worsening problem.

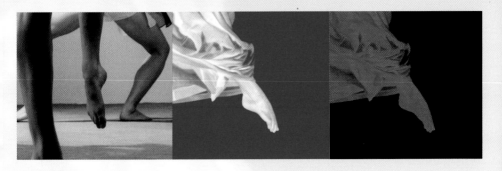

Overeating, dieting and bingeing

The early stages of an eating disorder can creep up on you by such ordinary steps that it's worth thinking about the connections between overeating, dieting and bingeing.

How do you know if you have overeaten? Is it because you feel bloated and uncomfortable and need to sleep off that large meal in front of the TV? Or is it because you feel angry at yourself for eating that extra piece of chocolate? Do you feel guilty because you have failed to keep your eating in check?

Everybody has experienced being over-full, after eating a large meal. Dieters know how they feel after failing to stick to their restrictive plan. Stomach fullness quickly disappears. Guilt, failure, and annoyance don't.

Controlling your eating for the sake of your weight or appearance (dieting) is fraught with difficulties. Every episode of eating is a challenge to your quota of calories. And once broken, diets are abandoned, for that day at least.

It's easy to interpret a single lapse in your plan as a total failure. So you give up and allow yourself to over-consume the food you were restricting.

But if you diet and overeat it's not the same as binge eating (or bingeing). You may think you have eaten much, much more than you should have, when you have actually only had a little extra. Diet breaking and binge eating are very different, but they are undeniably interconnected. In the majority of cases, bingeing has been preceded by dieting.

True binge eating disorder is characterised by a compulsion to eat huge amounts of food. You eat rapidly during a binge, and you feel out of control either before or during the binge. Binge eating almost certainly results in weight gain and therefore, in weight conscious people such as dancers, is more likely to develop into bulimia nervosa. *(See 'Eating disorders' and for more advice contact the Eating Disorders Association, listed in 'Advice, information and support')*

Eating disorders

Anorexia nervosa and *bulimia nervosa* are the two medically defined eating disorders that are most likely to affect dancers. They can often be interdependent and dancers may start with one that then develops into the other.

Anorexia Nervosa

The strict medical definition of anorexia nervosa centres on having a too-low body weight and therefore suffering from hormonal upsets. But, the key factor is the determination to pursue weight loss and avoid any possibility of weight gain.

If you have anorexia, food is never off your mind. You count calories all the time and keep reducing your daily total allowance. You may limit the grams of fat you are allowed each day and it will always be a shrinking number.

You might avoid eating a proper meal. People see you eating snacks - even chocolate occasionally - but you find the idea of a substantial meal terrifying. You might only allow yourself a certain number of foods each day, or avoid some foods altogether. Bread, potatoes, pasta and any food containing fat disappear from your diet while you try to fill the gap with low fat cottage cheese and piles of chopped lettuce, cabbage and carrot.

"I wanted to look so perfect as a dancer - it all went horribly wrong. Small wasn't small enough - 6½ stone went to 4½ and at my worst down to 3½ - so you eat less in the hope of achieving that 'high' and that perfection. In my search for body perfection I've ended up a skeletal wreck too fragile to touch. Nobody wants this body. How could anybody love this? It's just not worth it. I've lost everything and wish I'd never started."
Julie Stanton

Maybe you skip meals. You rarely eat with other people so you become isolated, tense and anxious. Your friends find you moody. Your sleep becomes disturbed. You are snappy and nothing is easy or fun any more. Persisting on this path brings exhaustion, loneliness, weakness and loss of hope for anything better. The despair can prompt suicide or the starvation can kill. Every year people die of anorexia nervosa. Others become chronically ill.

You may start to vomit after eating. You feel that even the little bit you allow yourself to eat needs to be got rid of. Sometimes anorexics can't maintain their low weight and it comes closer to normal levels but they still feel anxious about food and vomiting may lead to bingeing and vomiting. *(See 'Bulimia Nervosa')*

What should I look out for?

Behavioural clues

- You cut food into tiny pieces and push them around your plate.
- You weigh yourself several times a day.
- You exercise excessively and avoid sitting down.
- You are hyperactive or constantly restless. You have poor, broken sleep.
- You wear big baggy clothes and lots of layers.
- You vomit or take laxatives.
- You are secretive about what and where you have eaten.

Physical clues

- As a teenager: you don't grow and your friends overtake you. You need to eat to grow.
- As an adult: you lose weight and need to buy clothes in smaller sizes.
- As a man: you lose your sex drive, your interest in sex, and have difficulty in maintaining an erection/or you don't get a morning erection.
- As a woman: your periods don't start or become irregular and then vanish. (This sign can be masked when you use the contraceptive pill.) You lose your sex drive.
- You are constipated and have abdominal pains, especially if you are not drinking enough fluid.
- You have low blood pressure which can make you dizzy when you sit up or stand up.
- Your skin, hands and feet are always cold and often look bluish or purple.
- You grow pale downy hair on the body - particularly the face, chin and back.

- Your stomach, face, feet, ankles and hands can suddenly appear swollen due to fluid retention. Gravity causes the fluid to collect in whatever part of the body is lowest - so you have puffy eyes in the morning and swollen feet and ankles at night. The swellings can be dented by finger pressure and the dents don't disappear when you stop pressing. Fluid retention can cause a misleading weight increase. It needs to be shown to a doctor.
- Your skin is dry, rough, and discoloured, Minor cuts or scratches take a long time to heal.

Psychological clues

- You are a perfectionist. You feel that nothing you do is good enough.
- You have an intense fear of gaining any weight - even 0.25 kg / 1/2 lb is a disaster.
- You feel fatter or bigger than the scales or other people say you are.
- You deny there's a problem and insist that, "I'm fine" when you're not.
- Your personality changes as obsessions with food grow and mood swings increase.

As well as looking after yourself, you should look after your friends too. Can you see any of the above signs in your friends? If you are concerned that a friend has anorexia talk sensitively to them about what you've noticed and seek advice from someone you trust. *(See 'What can I do now?')*

You can get better

You can break your starvation pattern with the right support. You won't be able to do it alone and will power isn't enough. It will take time. You'll have to learn how to eat more, and to eat healthily. You will need courage to face the fears that hold you back. It won't be easy, but getting your life back will be worth the struggle. *(See 'What can I do now?')*

Bulimia Nervosa

If you have bulimia, you feel out of control around food which leads to repeated binges when very large amounts of food are eaten in a short time. After bingeing, you then try to reduce any possible weight gain by throwing up, taking laxatives, exercising fiercely or attempting to fast. The medical definition of bulimia requires that binges are frequent and have taken place for a sustained period of time (for at least 3 months).

When it happens to you it feels much worse because you have lost control. Food alone can't satisfy your hunger. But you still binge. You have an uncontrollable urge to eat, getting through whole loaves of bread, packets of cake or biscuits, or cereal in just one binge. You eat everything in the house because you can't stop until it's all gone. You eat thousands of calories and then drink litres of fizzy drink to help you to vomit them up afterwards.

Bingeing becomes a dustbin for your bad feelings. When you feel worried by fear, guilt, panic or loneliness, you eat as much as you can. But then guilt sets in. You immediately throw up or swallow laxatives (or both). When these have worked you might find temporary relief in exhausted sleep.

Whatever happens you feel you can't gain weight. Tomorrow you might be able to dance off those extra calories. Or the compulsion to binge may strike again.

In front of friends you manage to make your eating appear normal. They don't notice you rush to the toilet after every time you eat. But binges dominate more and more of your evenings when you are alone at home. You come to dread interruptions which could lead to the discovery of your guilty secret.

Laxatives don't stop you absorbing what you have eaten. Laxatives work on the large bowel. By the time waste matter gets there what can be absorbed has already been absorbed earlier on in the passage through the gut. What laxatives do is to make you short of mineral electrolytes like potassium. If you don't have enough of these electrolytes in your body, muscle contraction and nerve conduction become inefficient. Low potassium concentrations in your body can cause sudden physical effects. You could collapse due to sudden muscle weakness or your heart could even stop beating.

Even being sick doesn't stop you absorbing some of the calories you have eaten. A proportion will have already been absorbed into the body by the time you throw up. If you keep vomiting you'll lose essential minerals such as potassium and sodium. Potassium and sodium keep your muscles functioning and you dancing.

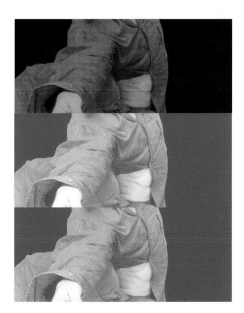

Bulimia can take over your life. You feel trapped by an overwhelming fear of becoming fat because you can't control your eating. You're ashamed of bingeing and lying - you feel inadequate, unattractive, worthless, moody and irritable.

Sometimes you feel OK. At other times you feel suicidal.

"Very soon I was throwing up my breakfast, which I thought was an act of genius, because it meant I had all the fun of eating and none of the worry of weight gain... [I] discovered the wonders of laxatives which I used on those days when there was nothing left in my stomach to bring up but green bile... I was very ill and unrecognisable in both body and mind... and I became a loner as a result of the elaborate lies I told and the secrets I kept."
Kate Thornton
'I was an anorexic', Marie Claire.

A full version of the article is available in the June 2000 issue of *Marie Claire*.

What should I look out for?

Behavioural clues

- You experience increasing dietary chaos. You eat what you never meant to eat and you fly to the toilet to throw up.
- Binges make you late or miss appointments.
- You feel ashamed of bingeing and lying about it. You become moody and irritable.
- You exercise excessively in sudden bouts.
- You are unwilling to have meals with friends or family.
- You avoid restaurants.
- You spend lots of money on food for binges. This may lead you into debt.
- You take food from shops and walk off without paying.
- You get so desperate you pick food out of waste bins to eat.

Physical clues

- You find it hard to concentrate.
- Your weight changes frequently.
- You have irregular periods.
- Your skin is in poor condition.
- Your teeth and gums are sensitive to heat and cold because dentine has been worn away by excessive vomiting.
- You have abrasions on the knuckle of the first finger where it catches on front teeth when you push your fingers down your throat to induce vomiting.
- You have swollen salivary glands which can make your face look wider from cheekbone to cheekbone.
- You are always tired.

Psychological and emotional clues

- You have uncontrollable urges to eat vast amounts of food.
- You are obsessed with food.
- You have a distorted perception of your body weight and shape.
- You are overemotional and have mood swings.
- You are anxious and depressed. You have low self-esteem, and feel ashamed and guilty.
- You feel isolated, helpless and lonely.

As well as looking after yourself, you should look after your friends too. Can you see any of the above signs in your friends? Or maybe food disappears overnight from a friend's cupboard or the shared fridge? If you are concerned that a friend has bulimia talk sensitively to them about what you've noticed and encourage them to seek advice from someone they trust. *(See 'What can I do now?')*

Long-term

Like anorexia, bulimia can take over your life. It can make you feel trapped and desperate. Bulimia might not be as visible as anorexia, but it is just as dangerous:

- Low potassium can cause muscle weakness or affect your heart beat.
- Kidney stones can be a long-term result of the recurrent dehydration that follows frequent vomiting.
- Worst of all, is the self-hatred and depression that poisons the way you view yourself.

You can get better

The symptoms of bulimia may have taken years to develop. But once you recognise them, you can get the right support and treatment straight away to help you break the pattern.

Self-help books can be useful. For example, they can show you how to keep a 'food and feelings diary' which can pinpoint the trouble spots that kick off the binges. *(See 'Some useful reading' in 'Advice, information and support')* But don't try and do this alone; books aren't the whole solution. You will need expert help and support to get better.

Recovery can be a very confusing time. It's easy to blame yourself or others. But remember, it's no one's fault. Once you find someone who can help and start a new eating pattern you can recover. *(See 'What can I do now?')*

If you are worried that your eating is disordered, this questionnaire can be a quick way to check on your eating patterns.

The SCOFF questionnaire

➔   Do you make yourself **S**ick because you feel uncomfortably full?

➔   Do you worry you have lost **C**ontrol over how much you eat?

➔   Have you lost more than **O**ne stone (7 kg) in a three-month period?

➔   Do you believe yourself to be **F**at when others say you are too thin?

➔   Would you say that **F**ood dominates your life?

If you have answered yes to two or more questions you may have an eating disorder. Please note that the questionnaire is only a guide. It you think you have an eating disorder, it's important to get advice from your GP, counsellor or the Eating Disorders Association helpline. *(See 'What can I do now?' and 'Advice, information and support')*

Morgan JF, Reed F, Lacey JH - 'The SCOFF Questionnaire', British Medical Journal, December 1999, 319:1467-1468. Published with permission from the BMJ Publishing Group.

What can I do now?

Eating disorders start out as solutions to a problem. The most obvious problem is that you feel too fat. But eating behaviours get used to solve other problems. You use your eating (or not eating or vomiting and purging) to deal with your life. You may eat less than you need because you feel bad about yourself. You may binge and vomit because you feel angry and upset. Maybe you haven't done as well as you would like, so you punish yourself through starvation.

But there are better ways to deal with difficult feelings than harming yourself through the way you use food:

- Share your problems with other people. Talk about your feelings.
- Don't bottle things up. Express the way you feel. Let yourself cry if you're upset and shout if you're angry.

First steps

If you recognise some of the signs of an eating disorder - in yourself or in a classmate or a company member - you may be unsure what to do next. You may feel that you daren't say anything in case you have to stop dancing. You may be afraid that you will lose your company place. You may not want to cause trouble for your friend. You may worry about handing over control of your eating.

The first step is to talk to someone - someone you trust and you feel comfortable with - a friend, teacher, company member or counsellor.

You're probably scared of admitting having a problem. You may think that the problem is a secret, but it's likely that your friends, teachers or company members have already guessed that something is wrong. They may have noticed your thinness, your declining performance, or your constant tiredness. You may also worry about how those around you will react. This is normal.

You need to talk to someone who understands, who won't judge you or take control; who will see you as a person, not just as a performer; and who understands your need to dance. It could be someone at your school or in your company. It might be your GP. But you may feel awkward - maybe you don't know your GP very well, or they may have known you since your childhood. Perhaps you would rather talk to someone anonymously on a helpline.

It can be harder for men to seek help. You may find it hard to talk about your feelings, problems and weight loss with other people. But your eating patterns can become deeply rooted and your body starved while you stay silent.

"It's more difficult to come forward, you can't admit to your feelings in a macho culture; people think you're weak and you fear that you're going to lose respect from your friends."
Male dancer

It's easier than you think

Asking for help isn't easy. The first step can be the hardest. You'll have to accept that you're struggling with an eating disorder and explore, understand and resolve the underlying issues and feelings.

But you can't do this on your own, no matter how determined you may be. It was your resolve and belief in your ability to control your body and life (and the planning it took) which led to your eating becoming disordered. Once the energy and belief trapped in anorexia-bulimia begins to be released back into dance and other areas of your life, you'll recover your old self.

What help is available?

It's never too late. Having an eating disorder isn't your fault. But it won't just go away. You need to be able to talk to someone in a positive environment who will give you advice, and point you in the direction of a counsellor or another qualified person; someone who will help you say what you need to say, and who won't judge you. If you're training or in a company you may be registered routinely with your GP. Or you could phone the Eating Disorders Association helpline which can give you the names of counsellors who can offer advice and help. *(See 'Advice, information and Support')*

If you are referred for specialist help, that help will only be effective if you are committed to getting better. The help that you receive should focus on your emotional and psychological well being as well as on your weight.

Help may be available through local mental health services, general psychiatric hospitals or specialist units. The help you receive should include:

- education on the consequences of eating disorders
- counselling or a form of psychotherapy
- monitoring of diet, weight and health
- support and information for carers and relatives

If you opt to go into an institution to receive support, the programme should provide:

- a safe environment
- continuing, consistent support from staff who understand the issues involved in eating disorders
- support during and after meals
- nutritional management and appropriate food
- ongoing counselling or psychotherapy

In extreme circumstances - when all other alternatives have failed - you could be detained under the Mental Health Act. This will only happen if your life is in danger or your eating behaviour is posing a severe risk to your health.

(The above information on treatment is adapted from the 'Anorexia and bulimia nervosa: information about treatment' leaflet produced by the Eating Disorders Association)

You're responsible for yourself and it's up to you to put your health first. If you have concerns or questions, it's important to speak out. Information and knowledge is your key. Seek the facts and ensure that when you're concerned or have a problem - whether it relates to you or someone you work with or are at school, college or university with - it's given appropriate attention and you get the help you need.

If you are a student

Schools, colleges and universities don't have an overall responsibility to look after your health and welfare. However, the board of directors or governors, through the principal and tutors, have some limited responsibilities for your health and welfare through your institution's internal rules and operations. For example, they do have a duty to provide you with a safe environment in which to train.

If you're worried, speak to a welfare adviser, a counsellor or a similar person. Most colleges and universities have welfare advisors, counsellors, personal tutors or similar people who you can talk to about any concerns you have. You should make it your business to find out who and where they are. If you can't find someone to talk to, ask any of your tutors who you should talk to if and when a problem arises. If you're stuck, your Student Union or the National Union of Students will have information on the best people or organisations that can help with you in your particular situation.

If you're not getting an appropriate response from one person, try someone else. *(See 'Advice, information and support')*

What people say to you
Does your school or training establishment have guidelines for the way teachers speak to you or give you feedback?

"The teacher told a girl in the group that she was getting 'chunky', actually violating rules about teachers' behaviour that were agreed upon in staff meetings as part of a prevention program. The particular rules that this teacher violated were that teachers were not allowed to make comments about their students' body shapes, and that they were not allowed to treat students' bodies disrespectfully. Indignantly, the girl responded by telling the teacher that she was in growth spurt and that restricting her nutritional intake at this time could threaten both her health and her growth."

© 1999. From *'Preventing Eating Disorders - A Handbook of Interventions and Special Challenges'* by Piran N, Levine MP and Steiner-Adair C. Reproduced by permission of Taylor & Francis, Inc., http://www.routledge-ny.com

Does your school or training establishment believe you should look thinner to get a job or a particular role? And if so, does it put pressure on you to lose weight?

If this sounds familiar what can you do about it?

Your best route (and a more usual solution) is to approach your personal tutor, a teacher you trust, welfare adviser, or counsellor. Or the bodies who regulate your school, college or university - i.e. governors, the Council for Dance Education and Training (CDET) or the Conference of Drama Schools. They are there to help you.

Confidentiality

If you give your school (or any other organisation) confidential information it must be kept confidential and only accessible to those who require it for justifiable purposes. For example, if you tell the principal of your school, or a tutor, that you suffer from, or have in the past suffered from an eating disorder, it would be legitimate for them to tell people who teach you in case you aren't strong or well enough to dance. They may also insist you get a scan for osteoporosis.

But they should not tell others who have no clear responsibility in your training/well-being, external examiners, or prospective employers.

Confidential information should not be disclosed to any third party without your written consent. Where you're being educated by an institution in the public sector (i.e. not at a private school) they must also comply with the requirements of the new Human Rights Act under which they have a general obligation to respect your privacy and your right to freedom of expression.

They should not tell you to 'get help or get out'. It may be possible to argue that this is discriminatory and that it's therefore unlawful. But by and large it would be subject to your contract with the training institution. They should offer you appropriate help and support - perhaps counselling.

Increasingly, dance schools and colleges have a specific policy about their attitude to eating disorders. This is not obligatory, but it is good practice. If your course is accredited by the CDET it has to fulfil requirements about student support. The institution will be expected to be familiar with eating disorder management and prevention as part of this.

Your rights as a student are quite limited. Your main recourse in the event of any dispute is likely to be the fact that your school/organisation is in breach of contract. You have agreed to pay for your course and in return they have agreed to train you (safely or with due care). It could be argued that they have a contractual duty to look after your health and welfare. It would also be a breach of contract if they refused to train you on 'body discrimination' grounds - i.e. that it's safe for you to train, but they refuse to let you attend class or act in a very negative way because your body shape is 'not right'.

Your rights under the Data Protection Act 1998 are the same as for employees. See page 34.

Sex Discrimination 1975, Race Relations 1976 and Disability Discrimination 1998 Acts

Students are entitled not to be discriminated against by their college or by their tutor on the grounds of their sex, race or any disability they may have. See 'Disability Discrimination Act 1998' on page 35 for a wider interpretation of disability. However, under the Disability Discrimination Act your training establishment is exempt from having to make adjustments to the workplace or to working practices in order to accommodate your disability.

It's up to you too

Your school, college or university has a duty to you to ensure that their premises are safe and free from hazards. As a trainee you too have a duty to notify your dance school, college or university of any hazards which you're aware of - such as broken floor boards or lack of heating. If they fail to take corrective action, you're entitled to refuse to continue to dance, rehearse, take class or work until your safety can be assured. Any dismissal or adverse treatment you receive as a result of you exercising your rights to work in a safe environment is illegal.

Risk assessments

Your school, college or university has a legal obligation to ensure that they follow safe working practices. In order to monitor this they must undertake risk assessments, and make any changes necessary to ensure that they comply with the law. For example, a teacher must know which exercises are safe to teach and which are potentially harmful, particularly if you're suffering from an eating disorder. They must take into account all relevant factors in a risk assessment including the fact you're suffering from an eating disorder. If you don't tell them they won't be aware of it so can't take it into account. Your best course of action may be to tell them but to make clear that it's on the basis that they'll keep it strictly confidential.

Safe working practices can cover a range of areas, for example: ensuring that you have had sufficient training in order to undertake a particular move, routine or piece of choreography; that it isn't contraindicated (or potentially harmful); that due care and attention is paid to how it's rehearsed (such as the number of repetitions); that there are suitable rest breaks and that the environment you're training, rehearsing or performing in is suitable.

Casting policies

If weight is an issue within castings, competitions or festivals, it is the company or panel's decision. You have no rights as an individual dancer.

Note: The sex, race and disability discrimination rights apply to casting, unless there are genuine reasons, such as authenticity.

Professional associations are beginning to devise or add to casting policies with specific reference to disordered eating. For example, The Prix de Lausanne is committed to advancing both health and excellence in tandem, in dancers. Potential candidates are required to complete a questionnaire in partnership with their family doctor, which screens for eating disorders, growth problems and anatomical risks. When the results indicate potential health risks, the Prix's consulting physician contacts those dancers and their physicians, urging them to seek solutions which will both improve the dancer's health and ultimately their performance. Dancers identified at this stage, or when they arrive in Lausanne, whose health would be compromised by the rigours of the competition are not allowed to participate.

If you're in some form of employment (including self-employment) - i.e. in a dance company or doing a show or summer season - and you're aged sixteen to eighteen you're entitled to most of the rights outlined below. If you're over eighteen you're entitled to them all.

Are you an employee?

The board of directors or governors, through their artistic directors, tutors and company administrators are responsible for your health and welfare.

What people say to you

"Some years ago I was told 'Careful that you don't gain weight during the summer holidays.' With a tap on the side of my hip, the ballet master dismissed me to contemplate the prospect of staying away from food for the next five weeks."
Cynthia Harvey

If this sounds familiar, what can you do about it?

Unless you can argue that the language amounts to sexual harassment, sexual discrimination or disability discrimination there's not much you can do legally. You should remember though that your health is of utmost importance.

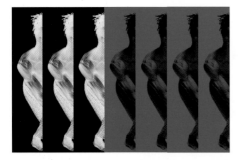

Confidentiality

If you give your employer (or any other organisation) confidential information, it must be kept confidential and only accessible to those who require it for justifiable purposes. For example, if you tell a choreographer, ballet master or company director that you suffer from, or have in the past suffered from an eating disorder, it would be legitimate for them to tell people who teach you in case you aren't strong or well enough to dance. They may also insist you get a scan for osteoporosis or that a doctor certifies that you're fit for the activities which you will be required to undertake.

They should not tell prospective employers. But, at the same time, they have a duty not to be misleading when talking to a prospective employer.

Sensitive personal information should not be disclosed to any third party without your written consent.

The circumstances where an employer could disclose confidential information about you are likely to be very limited.

The Data Protection Act 1998

You're entitled to see all information or records - paper or electronic - held about you. It's illegal for anyone to use your sensitive personal data (e.g. details of your health, ethnicity, sexuality) for any purpose other than one for which you have given written authorisation. Even your doctor can't disclose any information concerning your health without your written consent (apart from to other doctors).

Sex Discrimination 1975 & Race Relations 1976 Acts

Employees have the right not to be discriminated against on the grounds of their sex, race or any disability they may have. See below for a wider interpretation of disability.

Disability Discrimination Act 1998

This prevents discrimination against anyone who is disabled. The concept of disability is a wide one, extending beyond the registered disabled to any illness or disability which has long-term effect (e.g. of one year or more) on your ability to undertake everyday activities. For example, disability can include:

- osteoporosis
- eating disorders (depending on its severity and its impact on your ability to undertake everyday activities such as class, rehearsals or performance)
- clinical depression or
- being HIV positive

It's up to you too

Ensuring health and safety is a duty of an employer. As an employee you also have a duty to notify your employer of any hazards that you're aware of such as broken floor boards or lack of heating. If your employer fails to take corrective action, you're entitled to refuse to continue to dance, rehearse, take class or work until your safety can be assured. Any dismissal or adverse treatment you receive as a result of you exercising your rights to work in a safe environment is illegal.

Risk assessments

Employers have a legal obligation to ensure that they offer safe working practices. In order to monitor this they must undertake risk assessments, and make any changes necessary to ensure that they comply with the law. For example, a ballet master or mistress, tutor or choreographer must know which exercises or moves are safe to teach and which are potentially harmful, particularly if you're suffering from an eating disorder. They must take into account all relevant factors in a risk assessment including the fact you're suffering from an eating disorder. If you don't tell them they won't be aware of it so can't take it into account. Your best course of action may be to tell them but to make clear that it's on the basis that they'll keep it strictly confidential.

Safe working practices can cover a range of areas. For example: ensuring that you have had sufficient training in order to undertake a particular move, routine or piece of choreography; that it isn't potentially harmful; that due care and attention is paid to how it's rehearsed (such as the number of repetitions); that there are suitable rest breaks and that the environment you're training, rehearsing or performing in (i.e. the condition of premises, floor, temperature and light) is suitable.

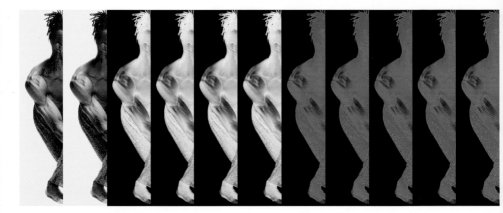

If you're taking part in a potentially dangerous site-specific project (i.e. on location, filming, rehearsing or performing in a non-theatre or studio environment), and you're concerned, you should ask if a risk assessment has been undertaken. If the company or organisation refuses to do one, or to voluntarily disclose the results, you should contact your union and/or the Health and Safety Executive. An employer's overall obligation to provide safe working practices requires them to consider the differing environments in which they may ask their dancers to work and having in place a process to ensure that the safety in these locations is considered.

This is particularly important if you have an eating disorder or osteoporosis as the risk to you may be greater.

Working time

There is now legislation in force that governs the maximum amount of time which employees can be required to work, although it's subject to exceptions.

You can agree to contract out of or waive some of the rights. However the position is very complex and professional bodies are fighting to try and prevent pressure from employers for people to contract out of their rights.

But not all of the rights can be contracted out of such as the right to four weeks' holiday and some of the rest periods.

There are minimum requirements for working hours and rest breaks, which can be especially relevant if you're rehearsing and/or touring, these are:

- a maximum working week of forty-eight hours (you may be asked to waive your right, if you refuse you can't be sacked)
- a minimum of forty-eight hours' rest every fortnight
- a minimum twenty-minute rest break every six hours
- a minimum of eleven consecutive hours' rest everyday; and
- a minimum of four weeks' paid holiday for all employees once they've completed thirteen weeks of service

The restrictions for employees aged fifteen to eighteen are stricter than those set out above.

Sick leave and sick pay

Generally, there's no need to have made National Insurance contributions in order to be entitled to sick pay, however it's wise to check with your employer to be sure that you qualify for sick pay.

As an employee you may have the right not to be dismissed on the grounds of sickness. If you have a disability which qualifies under the Disability Discrimination Act (see page 35) you will have protection. However, it's not necessarily unlawful to sack someone for their inability to undertake the work for which they were originally engaged. The better course of action would be to try and find a different job for them to do. But if you have a long-term illness which makes it impossible for you to do the job for which you were employed, i.e. as a dancer, you may be legally dismissed by your employer if there's no alternative job which you could do. An appropriate alternative might be to find a non-performing role for you as a dancer if you can't perform due to your disordered eating or you have an injury such as a stress fracture or osteoporotic fracture. You could be offered some company administration or stage management. If you refuse to accept it your employer may be able to dismiss you.

Casting policies

Some of the trade associations, such as the Independent Theatre Council, which has a number of small and medium scale performance and educational companies in its membership, have policies of best practice in casting. Although organisations aren't usually obliged to adopt these policies, many choose to do so and often include some form of non-discriminatory approach to casting, in terms of sex, appearance etc., to the extent that this is possible.

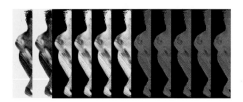

Professional associations are beginning to devise or add to casting policies with specific reference to disordered eating.

If weight is an issue within castings, competitions or festivals, it is the company or panel's decision. You have no rights as an individual dancer.

Whistle-blowing

As an employee you're entitled to statutory protection from dismissal or adverse treatment if you notify an external organisation of your concerns about the legality or safety of working practices, providing that you aren't acting maliciously. However, you are only protected if you have raised your concerns with your employer first, and your employer has still not acted.

Statutory protection potentially may cover notifying an external agency of an employer's approach to treating staff with eating disorders.

Your employer will breach their overall legal obligation if, for example, you were sacked because you went to an external agency such as The Disability Rights Commission.

Statutory protection isn't designed to cover an individual telling an employer about a colleague who has an eating disorder.

Some of the rights outlined above will also depend on your status - as an employee or a freelancer.

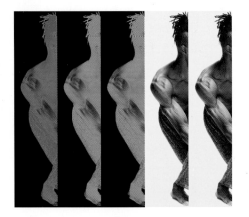

If you are self-employed and generate work for others

If you're self-employed but generating work for other self-employed dancers you should ensure that you take appropriate care of those dancers and you may also be obliged to take out employer's liability insurance. If you're in any doubt, you should seek advice from your trade union or one of the trade associations. **(See 'Advice, information and support')**

If you are self-employed

Your rights
Confidentiality, data protection, and sex, race and disability discrimination legislation applies between yourself as a self-employed dancer, choreographer or teacher and the person to whom you provide your services.

If you're self-employed/freelance you're your own employer, you need to:

- look after your own body
- be responsible for looking after yourself - your own healthcare, tax affairs, pension, etc.

As a freelancer/self-employed person you are not covered by employment law, just contract law.

If you have several jobs

Like many dance professionals, you may do several jobs to make a living. For some of these jobs you may be employed on PAYE, and at the same time for others you may be contracted as self-employed/freelance.

For more information on understanding contracts see Dance UK's publications 'The Dancers' Survival Guide' and Information Sheet 9.

Getting the right legal advice

It's essential to get detailed legal advice on your particular circumstance. Often the detail of these rights can be complicated and you may need someone to help guide you through the issues. Welfare or legal advisers at your trade union are often a good place to start.

Prevention is easier than cure

This booklet provides lots of suggestions for keeping healthy. The key points are:

- Be the best dancer you can be. This means looking after your body, giving it enough fuel and enjoying its achievements.

- There is no absolute, ideal body shape. Different dance styles, cultures and choreographers emphasise different shapes and other qualities in their dancers.

- Don't become obsessed with the mirror. Enjoy the physical sensation of dancing.

- Create your own performance eating plan. Use the information provided in the *'Eating for health and performance'* section, and include lots of the healthy things that you enjoy.

- Be aware of the risks connected with disordered eating, amenorrhoea and osteoporosis and seek help and advice early if you are worried.

If you are worried

Talk to someone. It might be a friend, teacher or relative. Explain how you feel.

Get the information. There are lots of organisations that can help by giving you information. *(See 'Advice, information and support')*

Schools and companies

Increasingly, vocational dance schools and companies have a written policy that explains their attitude to managing eating disorders. The best ones include:

- Recognition of the risks for dancers.

- A commitment to promoting the health and well-being of their students.

- The action that will be taken to support students with eating disorders and to promote their recovery.

- Issues relating to confidentiality.

Make sure you are aware of any policy that your school or company might have.

"It's about quality and performance, not just physical shape. I've always been very interested in what you can do with training. It's about being strong, fit and healthy - and making the most of the dancer you are."
David Nixon, Artistic Director, Northern Ballet Theatre

Professional and legal advice & information

Please note that all these bodies can only give advice relating to the current situation in the UK.

Citizens Advice Bureaux
Free, confidential advice on a range of subjects.
You can find the contact details of your local Citizens Advice Bureau in your local telephone directory.

National Association of Citizens Advice Bureaux website:
www.nacab.org.uk

The Commission for Racial Equality
Information and advice on racial discrimination.
Telephone +44 (0)20 7828 7022
Website www.cre.gov.uk

The Council for Dance Education and Training
The UK's leading body representing professional dance training and related educational interests. General information service for those wanting to know about dance training.
Telephone +44 (0)20 7247 4030
Website www.cdet.org.uk

The Disability Rights Commission
Information on the Disability Discrimination Act
Telephone +44 (0)8457 622633
Website www.drc-gb.org

The Equal Opportunities Commission
Responsible for issues relating to sex equality and sex discrimination.
Telephone +44 (0)161 833 9244
Website www.eoc.org.uk

Equity
Trade union for professional performers
Telephone +44 (0)20 7379 6000
Website www.equity.org.uk

The Health and Safety Executive
Responsible for issues relating to health and safety at work.
Telephone +44 (0)8701 545500
Website www.hse.gov.uk

The Independent Theatre Council (ITC)
Management association for small and medium scale performance companies.
Telephone +44 (0)20 7403 1727
Website www.itc-arts.org

The Office of the Information Commissioner
Information on access to personal data.
Telephone +44 (0)1625 545745
Website www.dataprotection.gov.uk

Theatrical Management Association (TMA)
Management association for medium and large scale performance companies.
Telephone +44 (0)20 7557 6706
Website www.tmauk.org

Advice on health, diet and eating disorders

Eating Disorders Association
For help with eating disorders including anorexia nervosa, bulimia and binge eating.

First Floor Wensum House
103 Prince of Wales Road
Norwich
NR1 1DW

Helpline +44 (0)1603 621 414
open 9.00 am to 6.30 pm (weekdays)
Email info@edauk.com
Website www.edauk.com

National Osteoporosis Society
For information on bone health and osteoporosis.

Camerton
Bath BA2 0PJ

Telephone +44 (0)1761 471771
Email info@nos.org.uk
Website www.nos.org.uk

Dance UK
For information on any aspect of your heath, fitness and well-being as a dancer.

Battersea Arts Centre
London SW11 5TN

Telephone +44 (0)20 7228 4994
Email info@danceuk.org
Website www.danceuk.org

Some Useful Websites

Caring Online
http://caringonline.com

Eating Disorder Referral and Information Center
http://edreferral.com

Positive Voices
www.ednewsletter.com

Something Fishy
www.somethingfishy.org

Support, Concern and Resources for Eating Disorders (SCaRED)
http://www.eating-disorder.org

Some useful reading

Anorexia & Bulimia - Your Questions Answered.
Julia Buckroyd. Element, 1996.
ISBN 1-85230-776-5.

Eating Your Heart Out - Understanding and overcoming eating disorders
Julia Buckroyd. Optima, 1994 (revised ed.).
ISBN 0-09-181502-9.

Anorexia and Bulimia: How To Help
Marilyn Duker & Roger Slade.
Open University Press, 1988.
ISBN 0-335-098320-0.

Hunger Strike - The Anorectic's Struggle As A Metaphor For Our Age
Susie Orbach. Penguin, 1993 (revised ed.).
ISBN 0-14-016978-4.

Understanding Eating Disorders
Bob Palmer. Family Doctor Publication, 1996.
ISBN 1-898205-15-9.

Getting Better Bit(e) By Bit(e) - A Survival Kit for Sufferers of Bulimia Nervosa and Binge Eating Disorders
Ulrike Schmidt and Janet Treasure.
Lawrence Erlbaum Associates, 1993.
ISBN 0-86377-322-2.

Helping Athletes With Eating Disorders
Ron A Thompson & Roberta Trattner Sherman. Human Kinetics Publishers, 1993.
ISBN 0873223837.

Fit but Fragile
National Osteoporosis Society.

The Fit and Healthy Dancer
Yiannis Koutedakis & NC Craig Sharp.
John Wiley & Sons, 1999.
ISBN 0-471-97528-1.

Useful publications from Dance UK

The Dancers' Survival Guide
Scilla Dyke (editor). Produced by Dance UK in collaboration with The Foundation for Community Dance and The Place Dance Services. Dance UK, 1999.
ISBN-0-9515631-5-7.

A Dancers' Charter for health and welfare
Dance UK, 7th ed., 1998.

Dance UK Information Sheets
Dance UK

1. *Finding a Medical or Complementary Health Practitioner*
2. *Dancer's First Aid Box*
3. *Warming Up and Cooling Down*
4. *Copyright for Dance*
5. *A Basic Guide to Insurance*
6. *Dance Floors*
7. *Care of the Instrument*
8. *Performing is Only a Stage in your Career*
9. *To PAYE or not to PAYE*
10. *Myths and Facts about Dance and the Body*
11. *How to have Healthy Bones*
12. *Food & Nutrition for Dancers*
13. *Muscular Imbalance Explained*
14. *'Burnout' in Dance*
15. *Fluids for Dancers*
16. *A Basic Guide to Pensions*
17. *What is Core Stability?*
18. *Dancers' Physical Therapy Questions Answered*

Your Body Your Risk

Key Contributions

Neil Adleman, Solicitor, Harbottle & Lewis

Steve Bloomfield, Media & Information Manager, Eating Disorders Association

Julia Buckroyd PhD, Psychotherapist (UKCP), Director of Studies for Counselling, University of Hertfordshire & Psychotherapist in private practice

Jasmine Challis BSc, SRD, Freelance Accredited Sports Dietician & Registered Nutritionist

Alan Currie MB, ChB, MPhil, MRCPsych, Consultant Psychiatrist, Honorary Lecturer in Neurosciences & Psychiatry, Newcastle City Health NHS Trust, Honorary Medical Officer, UK Athletics

Linda Edwards BA (Hons) Dip CAM MIPR, Director, National Osteoporosis Society

Alison Graham Assistant Communications Manager, National Osteoporosis Society

Andrew J Hill PhD CPsychol, Senior Lecturer in Behavioural Sciences, Academic Unit of Psychiatry & Behavioural Sciences, School of Medicine, University of Leeds

Nicola Keay MRCP, Research Endocrinologist, Kingston Hospital

Elizabeth Nabarro BSc (Hons) Psych; Psychotherapist (UKCP), Student Counsellor, London Contemporary Dance School & Psychotherapist in private practice

Mervat Nasser MD, MPhil, MRCPsych, Senior Lecturer & Consultant Psychiatrist, Leicester University

Sheelagh Rodgers BA (Hons) MSc, MBA, Diploma in Cognitive Therapy, Work at Stockton Hall York, Member British Olympic Associations Psychology Steering group, BASES accredited Sports Psychologist

Jessica Shenton, Consultant to Dance UK's Healthier Dancer Programme

Jill Welbourne MD, Patron, Eating Disorders Association

Roger Wolman MD FRCP, Consultant in Rheumatology and Sports Medicine, the Royal National Orthopaedic Hospital, London. Medical Officer, Rambert Dance Company & The British Olympic Medical Centre

Photography

Bill Cooper

Hugo Glendinning

Chris Nash

Eric Richmond

Tim Simmons

Peter Williams